T0398160

ARE THEY REAL?

THE LOCH NESS MONSTER

by Janie Havemeyer

BrightP★int Press

San Diego, CA

BrightPoint Press

© 2024 BrightPoint Press
an imprint of ReferencePoint Press, Inc.
Printed in the United States

For more information, contact:
BrightPoint Press
PO Box 27779
San Diego, CA 92198
www.BrightPointPress.com

LIBRARY OF CONGRESS CATALOGING-IN-PUBLICATION DATA

Names: Havemeyer, Janie, author.
Title: The Loch Ness monster / by Janie Havemeyer.
Description: San Diego, CA: BrightPoint, [2024] | Series: Are they real? | Includes
    bibliographical references and index. | Audience: Ages 13 | Audience: Grades 7-9
Identifiers: LCCN 2023012466 (print) | LCCN 2023012467 (eBook) | ISBN 9781678206321
    (hardcover) | ISBN 9781678206338 (eBook)
Subjects: LCSH: Loch Ness monster--Juvenile literature.
Classification: LCC QL89.2.L6 H38 2024 (print) | LCC QL89.2.L6 (eBook) | DDC 001.944--
    dc23/eng/20230407
LC record available at https://lccn.loc.gov/2023012466
LC eBook record available at https://lccn.loc.gov/2023012467

CONTENTS

AT A GLANCE

- The Loch Ness Monster is a creature that is believed to live in a lake called Loch Ness in Scotland.

- The monster is commonly described as a large marine creature with a long neck and tail. It is also believed to have humps on its back.

- Scotland has many old stories about water monsters, including kelpies and sea serpents.

- Some people believe the first reported sighting of the Loch Ness Monster came from an account written in 565 CE.

- Interest in the monster rose in the 1930s. This is because a creature similar to the Loch Ness Monster, known as *Elasmosaurus*, was featured in the 1933 movie *King Kong*.

- In 1933, a tourist named George Spicer was the first person to describe the Loch Ness Monster in modern times.

- Many people have claimed they have seen the monster or found evidence that it exists. But a lot of evidence has been proven to be fake.

- Some people believe the monster could be an ancient reptile called *Plesiosaurus*.

- Loch Ness has been searched using sonar technology. But no monster has ever been found.

- Belief in the Loch Ness Monster has made Loch Ness a huge tourist attraction. Many people travel there in hopes of finding the monster.

INTRODUCTION

THE MONSTER OF LOCH NESS

It was the afternoon of July 22, 1933. George Spicer was driving along the shore of Loch Ness, a lake in Scotland. Spicer's wife sat in the passenger seat. As the car went up a hill, a huge creature crossed the road. It looked about 25 to 30 feet (7.5–9 m) long. It had a long neck.

Spicer thought he also saw a long tail.

The creature was on the road for only a

few seconds. Then it disappeared behind

some bushes. Spicer slowed the car to

get a better look. But the creature had

There are several roads and walking trails that surround the shores of Loch Ness.

The village of Drumnadrochit in Scotland, which is located near Loch Ness, has a sculpture of what some people believe the Loch Ness Monster looks like.

vanished. All Spicer could see was a trail of trampled grass.

Spicer wrote to the local newspaper a few days later. The *Inverness Courier* reported on news around Loch Ness.

It published his letter. Spicer wrote, "I saw the nearest approach to a dragon or prehistoric animal that I have ever seen in my life."[1] He claimed the creature had gray skin "like a dirty elephant or rhinoceros."[2] Spicer was not sure what kind of creature he saw.

IS IT REAL?

Spicer's letter was the first description in modern times of how people picture the Loch Ness Monster. Earlier sightings had not described much about it. Fishers had seen giant splashes in the lake. One couple reported seeing something like a whale. But Spicer painted a clearer picture. After his letter was published, a wave of new monster sightings poured in.

Many people have claimed to have seen the Loch Ness Monster since 1933. But eyewitness reports are not solid evidence. None of the monster's bones, teeth, or other remains have been found. Many people continue to look for evidence. They want to find out what kind of animal is being seen. They want proof that the Loch Ness Monster exists. Could the Loch Ness Monster be real?

Photographs and videos that claim to be of the Loch Ness Monster are often found to be fake.

1
WHAT IS THE LOCH NESS MONSTER?

The Loch Ness Monster is said to be a large **marine** monster. It is believed to live in the waters of Loch Ness in Scotland. The monster is also sometimes called Nessie.

Spicer's description of the Loch Ness Monster is how it is commonly pictured

today. People describe the Loch Ness

Monster as a large reptilelike creature.

Reports of the monster say it is around

20 feet (6 m) long. The Loch Ness Monster

is believed to have a long neck and tail. It is

Interest in finding proof of the Loch Ness Monster's existence grew in the 1930s.

also described as having flippers that allow it to swim. The monster is sometimes said to be a gray or green color. There are also several reports of it having one or more large humps on its back.

However, descriptions of the Loch Ness Monster are sometimes different from one another. Tim Dinsdale was an engineer who searched for the monster. He said, "Everyone seemed to have noted a different number of 'humps' in the water—one, two, three, and even more on occasions, and sometimes no humps at all, just a huge back like an upturned boat."[3]

Scotland is home to tens of thousands of lakes, but Loch Ness is one of the most famous because of the Loch Ness Monster.

THE MONSTER'S HOME

Loch Ness is located in northern Scotland.

It is near the city of Inverness. *Loch* is a

Scottish word. It means "inland lake." Loch

Ness is the second-largest lake in Scotland.

It is also one of the country's deepest lakes. The lake is 22 miles (35 km) long. It is as deep as 788 feet (240 m). The lake water is not very clear. The soil around the loch is filled with **peat**. This topsoil ends up in the water. It makes it hard to see below the surface. The water temperature is also very cold. It is usually around 40°F (4°C).

Loch Ness has always been a popular place to visit. And for many years, there were no reports of a monster. But that changed in 1930. A news story in a local paper reported a terrible noise coming from the water.

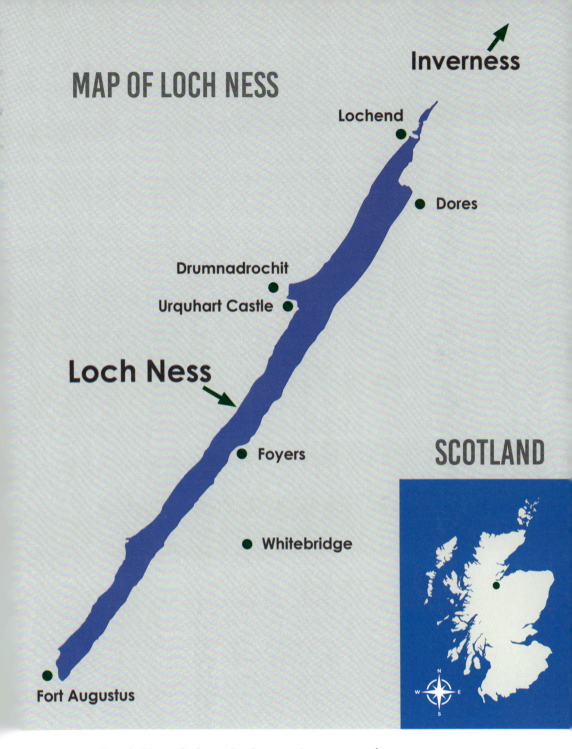

MAP OF LOCH NESS

Inverness

Lochend

Dores

Drumnadrochit

Urquhart Castle

Loch Ness

Foyers

SCOTLAND

Whitebridge

Fort Augustus

Loch Ness is located near Inverness in northern Scotland.

Some reports of Loch Ness Monster sightings include people hearing or seeing big water splashes.

THE LEGEND TAKES SHAPE

The *Northern Chronicle* reported on news in Inverness. One day in 1930, the newspaper featured an article about a strange event on Loch Ness. Three men were fishing. Suddenly, they heard a loud noise. It came from a wild splashing. The splashing caused a big wave to rock their boat. One of the fishers was named Ian Milne. He said, "We had no idea what it was, but we are quite positive it could not have been a salmon."[4]

Another paper, the *Kokomo Tribune*, also reported on the story. But it used the word *monster* to describe what could have made the splashing in the lake. The story from the *Kokomo Tribune* sparked the public's interest. A possible monster in the lake was exciting.

Another reporter also wrote about a monster in Loch Ness. The reporter's name was Alex Campbell. Campbell published an article in the *Inverness Courier* in 1933. He

titled it "Strange Spectacle on Loch Ness:

What Was It?" Campbell said the stories of

a scary monster living in Loch Ness were

real. He said the beast had been seen

again. The newspapers brought attention

CAPTAIN JOHN MACDONALD

John MacDonald was a steamship captain on Loch Ness. He wrote to the newspaper after reading Alex Campbell's article in 1933. MacDonald said he had never seen a monster. Over the course of fifty years, he had made around 20,000 trips up and down Loch Ness. MacDonald believed he would have seen the monster if it existed.

Eyewitness reports of the Loch Ness Monster are a common form of evidence used to prove its existence.

to the possibility of a monster living in

Loch Ness.

2
THE HISTORY OF THE LOCH NESS MONSTER

Stories of water monsters have been told for centuries. Scotland has a long history of belief in such monsters. Sailors would often return home with tales of monsters they had seen. These monsters were terrifying to locals. People in Scotland learned to be careful around water.

SCOTTISH WATER MONSTERS

Kelpies are evil spirits from Scottish **mythology**. They are water monsters believed to live near streams and rivers. Kelpies are said to change their shape.

Kelpies are also known as water horses.

They often look like horses. They do this to trick people into getting close to the water. Horses are gentle creatures. But kelpies attack and kill. They especially like to harm children.

Another type of water monster is known as an Each-Uisge (ack-ush-gay). It is similar to a kelpie. But it is said to live in the sea and lochs. The Each-Uisge changes shape too. Sometimes, it might look like a horse or pony. It can also look like a man. The creature will trap and drown its victims. Then it eats the bodies. The Each-Uisge hunts humans, cattle, and sheep. People

Stories about sea serpents have been told for centuries.

were often scared of animals and strangers

they met by the water's edge. They believed

the animals and strangers might be

shape-shifting water monsters.

There are also old Scottish **folktales**

about sea serpents. Sea serpents lived in

the sea and in lochs. One famous tale is of

Large logs or tree branches in the water can easily be mistaken as being the Loch Ness Monster.

a sea serpent called the Stronsay Beast.

It supposedly washed up on a Scottish

island called Stronsay in 1808. People

described it as "a sea-snake with a mane

like a horse."[5] The beast was brought to the

city of Edinburgh. Scientists examined it.

No one could figure out what it was. Finally, a man named Sir Everard Home believed he solved the mystery. He decided the beast was a shark.

FIRST RECORDED SIGHTING

A story from 565 CE is said to be the first written description of the Loch Ness Monster. The story was written by a **monk** called Adomnán in his book titled *The Life of Saint Columba*.

The book was about a real Irish monk named Columba who visited Scotland. One day, he stood on the shore of the

The water of Loch Ness is not very clear. Some people say that is how the Loch Ness Monster is able to stay hidden.

River Ness. The River Ness flows out

of Loch Ness. Columba wanted to cross

the river. As he was figuring out how to

cross it, he met a group of people. They

were burying a person who had been killed

by what they believed was a water beast.

Columba saw a boat on the other side of the river. He decided he could use it to cross the river. He asked another monk to go get the boat. The monk swam across the river. But his splashes woke the water beast. The beast rose up to attack. Columba yelled at the beast to try to stop it from attacking the monk. He shouted at it to go away. Columba's words worked. The water beast swam off. Columba had saved the monk.

It is impossible to know whether this story is true or not. The story was written one hundred years after Columba died.

The author, Adomnán, was not at the lake when the beast was seen. There are many reasons not to believe this tale. Still, people call this story the first tale of the Loch Ness Monster.

MONSTER FEVER

The Loch Ness Monster became very popular in the 1930s. This was a time when many people were thinking about monsters. It began with the release of the movie *King Kong* in 1933. The movie was a worldwide hit. It terrified everyone who saw it. *King Kong* is about a giant ape that is discovered

After the release of the movie King Kong, *the Loch Ness Monster was featured in several other movies and shows, such as* The Private Life of Sherlock Holmes *(pictured).*

in a remote jungle. But there is also a scary

lake monster featured in the movie. The

monster is called *Elasmosaurus*. It was

based on a prehistoric water reptile with a

long neck.

Rupert Gould wrote one of the first books about the Loch Ness Monster. It is called *The Loch Ness Monster and Others*. The book came out in 1934. Gould gathered reports from people who had claimed to see the monster. He interviewed George Spicer. Spicer said that he had

ELASMOSAURUS

Elasmosaurus was a type of plesiosaur that lived between 85 million and 65 million years ago. It was a large marine reptile with a long neck, similar to how the Loch Ness Monster is described today. *Elasmosaurus* is believed to have the longest neck of all plesiosaurs. The first fossil was discovered in 1868.

seen *King Kong* before his sighting of the Loch Ness Monster. Spicer described his monster as looking just like the lake monster in *King Kong*. Some people think the movie influenced Spicer. It was easier to imagine real-life monsters after seeing one on the big screen.

Ronald Binns studied the Loch Ness Monster. He wrote a book in 1984 called *The Loch Ness Mystery Solved*. He said, "It is probably no coincidence that the Loch Ness Monster was discovered at the very moment that King Kong . . . was released across Scotland."[6]

3

LOOKING AT THE
EVIDENCE

The Loch Ness Monster is a mysterious creature. Many people have tried to look for it. But no proof of the Loch Ness Monster has ever been found. Still, some people believe the monster exists. There have been many ideas about what kind of creature it could be.

THE *PLESIOSAURUS* THEORY

One common idea is that the Loch Ness

Monster is a *Plesiosaurus*. Plesiosauri

were prehistoric marine reptiles. They

lived between 215 million and 66 million

Plesiosauri were believed to live in the seas near Europe and around the Pacific Ocean.

years ago. They had long necks, small heads, and wide flippers. Plesiosauri were about 15 feet (4.5 m) long. They weighed around 1,000 pounds (450 kg).

Some people think that a *Plesiosaurus* is living in Loch Ness. But many scientists disagree. Plesiosauri lived in warm salt water. Loch Ness is a cold freshwater lake. There is also not enough food for plesiosauri to eat in the loch. Plesiosauri also need air to breathe. They must surface for air. This would make them easier to spot. No bones from this ancient reptile have been found in Loch Ness either.

PHOTOS AS EVIDENCE

Some people have claimed to photograph the Loch Ness Monster. The first known photo was taken by a man named Hugh Gray. He took it in 1933. Gray lived near Loch Ness. One day, he thought he saw the monster. Gray took five photos as evidence. Four photos showed nothing. The fifth

THE *VIPERFISH*

Don Taylor was an inventor and adventurer. He came to Loch Ness in 1969. Taylor brought his 20-foot (6-m) yellow submarine. He called it the *Viperfish*. Taylor used the submarine to explore Loch Ness. He searched for the Loch Ness Monster. But he never found evidence that the monster existed.

photo was very blurry. No one knew what Gray's photo really showed.

Another photograph of the Loch Ness Monster was published in a newspaper called the *Daily Mail*. They published it on April 21, 1934. It had been sent in by a doctor. His name was Robert Kenneth Wilson. Wilson's photograph was called the "Surgeon's Photograph."

The photo shows an unknown object sticking out of the water. To some people, it almost looked like a creature with a long neck. It was difficult to tell what the object in the water could actually be. But when

The "Surgeon's Photograph" was believed to be a real photo of the Loch Ness Monster because it was taken by a respected doctor.

the photo was published, many people believed it was a picture of the Loch Ness Monster. It became the most famous photo of the monster ever taken.

In 1975, a man named Ian Wetherell claimed the "Surgeon's Photograph" was a fake. He said the photo had been a trick created by Ian's father. His father was the well-known trickster Marmaduke Wetherell.

Marmaduke had built a small model monster using a toy submarine. Then he and his son drove to Loch Ness. Ian said, "We found an inlet where the tiny ripples would look like full size waves out of the loch."[7] The film was then passed on to a second man who gave it to Wilson. Wilson then sent one of the photos to the *Daily Mail*.

TIM DINSDALE'S FILM

The best evidence of the Loch Ness

Monster was taken with a movie camera.

Tim Dinsdale read an article about the Loch

Ness Monster in 1959. He was curious to

find out more about it. Dinsdale drove to

Loch Ness in the spring of 1960. He spent

many days there with his camera. On the

FOOTPRINTS ON THE SHORE

Marmaduke Wetherell claimed to have found the monster's footprints. His **cast** of the footprints was sent to a museum in London. Experts said they were fake. Wetherell had made the prints himself. He had made them by using an umbrella stand that was in the shape of a hippopotamus foot.

sixth day, Dinsdale believed he saw the monster. He used his movie camera to record his sighting. Dinsdale thought he had captured the monster on film. But scientists did not agree. The film was shot from far away. The creature looked like a fuzzy blob. Still, television audiences loved the film. It made Dinsdale into a celebrity. He became a well-known expert on the Loch Ness Monster.

Photographic experts from the United Kingdom's Royal Air Force studied Dinsdale's film in 1966. They enlarged the image. They decided the fuzzy blob was

Many tourists visit Loch Ness in hopes of capturing a picture of the monster.

not the Loch Ness Monster. They believed it

looked more like a motorboat.

THE LOCH IS SEARCHED

There have been many searches of Loch

Ness using sonar technology. A sonar

Sonar is used to look for objects underwater.

device sends out sound waves underwater. It listens for reflections. This tells the device where underwater objects are.

The first sonar **survey** of Loch Ness was done in 1962. Four boats used sonar to look for large objects in the loch. The team who did the search said, "Nothing was detected by any of the boats. This seems to rule out the possibility that a large animal exists in the body of Loch Ness."[8]

Still, sonar has continued to be used to look for the monster. The biggest sonar search was done in 1987. It was called Operation Deepscan. This search used twenty sonar boats to sweep the loch from end to end. The search discovered three large objects that could not be explained. However, no solid evidence of the Loch Ness Monster has been found using sonar.

EXPERTS WEIGH IN

Over the years, experts have proposed new ideas to explain the many sightings. Many experts agree that people mistake ordinary things for the monster. Tim Dinsdale also admitted this. He thought he saw the monster many times. But he realized that one sighting was actually a tree trunk. Another time he thought a swirl of waves looked like a big animal.

Some experts believe that the Loch Ness Monster could be a large gray seal. Loch Ness connects to the North Sea by the River Ness. Some experts wonder if seals swim from the North Sea into the lake. Gray seals have been seen in Loch Ness before. It is possible that the Loch Ness Monster could be a very large gray seal. But there

Male gray seals can grow up to 10 feet (3 m) long and weigh around 880 pounds (400 kg).

is no proof to confirm that. With no solid

evidence, people continue to search for the

Loch Ness Monster.

4

THE CULTURAL IMPACT OF THE LOCH NESS MONSTER

There are around 31,000 lochs in Scotland. Many of these lochs supposedly contain monsters of their own. There is Morag at Loch Morar. There is Lizzie at Loch Lochy. But the Loch Ness Monster is the most famous monster of them all.

BRINGING IN MONEY

The Loch Ness Monster is a major tourist

attraction in Scotland. Visitors come to Loch

Ness all year round. The monster makes

about $54 million for Scotland each year.

The ruins of Urquhart Castle overlook Loch Ness.

Tourists buy Loch Ness Monster products. They go on tours of the lake. They visit Loch Ness Monster exhibits. People are curious about the monster.

Travel companies sell train and bus tours around the Loch Ness area. They give tours and talk about the monster. The Loch Ness Monster has appeared in radio programs.

NESSIE HUNTER

Steve Feltham holds the world record for the longest time spent searching for the Loch Ness Monster. He is known as the Nessie Hunter. Feltham began his search in 1991. In 2016, he was recognized by *Guinness World Records* for his continuous search of the monster.

It has been in comic strips and movies. There have also been songs written about it. The monster's image sells products too. Some of the strangest products advertised using the monster have been mustard, floor polish, and breakfast cereal.

NESSIE IN THE MOVIES

The Loch Ness Monster has been featured in several movies since *King Kong*. One movie the monster was featured in was *The Private Life of Sherlock Holmes*. It was released in 1970. The movie is about the famous detective Sherlock Holmes

In the movie The Water Horse, the main character, Angus, names the legendary water horse he raises Crusoe.

searching for a missing person. The search

takes him to Loch Ness in Scotland. While

there, Holmes's partner, Dr. John Watson,

believes he sees the Loch Ness Monster.

A creature similar to the Loch Ness Monster is also featured in a children's movie. The movie is called *The Water Horse: Legend of the Deep*. It was released in 2007.

The movie is about a little boy from Scotland named Angus who finds a mysterious egg. The creature in the egg turns out to be a water horse, a creature from Scottish mythology. Angus and his family decide to release the creature into Loch Ness when it gets too big for them to keep. Some of the movie's events are based on famous reports of the Loch

Ness Monster.

THE LOCH NESS MONSTER IN THE 2000s

Around a million people visit Loch Ness

every year. About 85 percent of them

come for the Loch Ness Monster. People

will sometimes use modern technology to

MONSTER FAN CLUB

The Loch Ness Monster has an official fan club. It is based at Loch Ness. It is a club where fans can learn more about the famous monster. The club's website is called *Nessie on the Net!* It has a live webcam. Fans can try searching for the monster themselves.

look for the monster. Richard Mavor has a YouTube channel. It is called Richard Outdoors. In 2021, Mavor flew a **drone** over Loch Ness. Viewers noticed a large shape in the water. It was swimming just below the surface. People thought it could be the Loch Ness Monster.

A scientist named Neil Gemmel led a study of Loch Ness. His research was featured in the 2019 documentary *Loch Ness Monster: New Evidence*. Gemmel collected water samples from the lake. He wanted to see what creatures might be living there. All living creatures leave

Today, people continue to look for proof that the Loch Ness Monster exists.

a trace of their DNA in the water. DNA

is the molecule inside cells that contains

genetic information. Gemmel studied all his

samples. He discovered a lot of eel DNA. Gemmel thinks the Loch Ness Monster could be a giant eel. He says, "We've used science to add another chapter to Loch Ness."[9]

IS THE LOCH NESS MONSTER REAL?

Many people have looked for evidence that the Loch Ness Monster exists. But no solid proof has ever been found. People continue to search for answers about what could be hiding in Loch Ness. Many hope that one day someone will find proof that the Loch Ness Monster is real.

GLOSSARY

cast

an object made by pouring liquid into a mold and letting it harden

drone

an aircraft that does not have a pilot on board

folktales

stories typically passed down by word of mouth

marine

found in or produced by the sea

monk

a member of a religious community of men who live in a monastery

mythology

a set of stories or beliefs associated with a particular location or group of people

peat

material found in marshy or damp soil, made up of decomposing plants

survey

an examination of something to find out more about it

SOURCE NOTES

INTRODUCTION: THE MONSTER OF LOCH NESS

1. Quoted in Daniel Loxton and Donald R. Prothero, *Abominable Science! Yeti, Nessie, and Other Famous Cryptids*. New York: Columbia University Press, 2013, p. 130.

2. "1933, July 22: Mr. and Mrs. George Spicer's Loch Ness Encounter," *Anomalies*, n.d. http://anomalyinfo.com.

CHAPTER ONE: WHAT IS THE LOCH NESS MONSTER?

3. Quoted in Loxton and Prothero, *Abominable Science!*, p. 155.

4. Quoted in Loxton and Prothero, *Abominable Science!*, p. 127.

CHAPTER TWO: THE HISTORY OF THE LOCH NESS MONSTER

5. Quoted in Loxton and Prothero, *Abominable Science!*, p. 213.

6. Quoted in Loxton and Prothero, *Abominable Science!*, p. 129.

CHAPTER THREE: LOOKING AT THE EVIDENCE

7. Quoted in Loxton and Prothero, *Abominable Science!*, p. 146.

8. Quoted in Loxton and Prothero, *Abominable Science!*, p. 170.

CHAPTER FOUR: THE CULTURAL IMPACT OF THE LOCH NESS MONSTER

9. "Loch Ness Monster May Be a Giant Eel, Say Scientists," *BBC*, September 5, 2019. www.bbc.com.

FOR FURTHER RESEARCH

BOOKS

Abnormal Field Guides to Cryptic Creatures: The Loch Ness Monster. Chicago, IL: World Book, 2020.

Ken Karst, *Loch Ness Monster*. Mankato, MN: Creative Education, 2020.

Steve Kort, *What Do We Know About the Loch Ness Monster?* New York: Penguin Workshop, 2022.

INTERNET SOURCES

"Is the Loch Ness Monster Real?" *TPL Kids*, n.d. https://kids.tpl.ca.

"Loch Ness Monster Not a Dinosaur, Could Be a Giant Eel," *KidsNews*, September 8, 2019. www.kidsnews.com.au.

Charles Paxton, "The Loch Ness Monster: A Modern History," *Conversation*, May 12, 2022. https://theconversation.com.

WEBSITES

Loch Ness and Nessie
www.wildernessscotland.com/blog/loch-ness-moster/

The Wilderness Scotland website features information on the Loch Ness Monster and on Loch Ness. The site also has a map of Loch Ness and talks about different activities and attractions around the lake.

Myth or Monster?
https://blog.google/products/maps/myth-or-monster-explore
-loch-ness-with/

This blog post from Google Maps includes information about Loch Ness and includes a link for people to view Loch Ness virtually. The Google Maps "Street View" function takes viewers over the water and around the shores of the entire lake so they can search for the Loch Ness Monster themselves.

Sea Dragons and Other Monsters from the Deep
www.wcl.govt.nz/blogs/kids/index.php/2022/01/31/sea-
dragons-and-other-monsters-from-the-deep/

This blog from the Wellington City Libraries in New Zealand discusses mysterious underwater monsters, including the Loch Ness Monster. The site features photographs, videos, books, and links about these creatures and the ocean.

INDEX

IMAGE CREDITS

ABOUT THE AUTHOR

Janie Havemeyer is an author of many books for young readers. Janie has a master's degree in education and taught in schools. Janie lives in San Francisco, California. She visited Scotland when she was seventeen and learned all about the Loch Ness Monster.